A true story from the Bible

Everybody wanted to see Jesus

so he could help them
and pray for them.

Some boys and girls
just like you came to see Jesus.

But Jesus's friends said,
"You're too little."

"Jesus can't talk to you."

And someone said, "Jesus is TOO busy!"

And someone else said,

"Jesus is TOO important!"

And someone else said ...

"STOP!"

"Wait a minute."

"Haaaaaang on ..."

"Let those little ones come here.
STOP getting in their way!"

Who was it?

It was Jesus!

great, big,

Jesus said,
   "You don't have to be a

"God is friends with you

if you know you are

just little and need his help."

... is that you?

Notes for grown-ups

This story comes from Mark 10 v 13-16. The disciples wanted to stop people bringing their children to Jesus, but this is what he said: *"Let the little children come to me, and do not hinder them, for the kingdom of God belongs to such as these. Truly I tell you, anyone who will not receive the kingdom of God like a little child will never enter it"* (v 14-15, NIV).

Jesus wants us to be his friends, and to follow him as King of our lives (that's what "receiving the kingdom of God" means). But you don't have to pay to enter God's kingdom, and you can't earn it by being good. As this story tells us, *"You don't have to be a great, big, super-good, important person to be God's friend"*. Instead it's like a little child getting a present. It's a free gift.

Jesus welcomes everyone who comes to him like a child and puts their trust in him.

Mark 10 v 13-16

(The Bible: New International Version)

¹³ People were bringing little children to Jesus for him to place his hands on them, but the disciples rebuked them. ¹⁴ When Jesus saw this, he was indignant. He said to them, "Let the little children come to me, and do not hinder them, for the kingdom of God belongs to such as these. ¹⁵ Truly I tell you, anyone who will not receive the kingdom of God like a little child will never enter it." ¹⁶ And he took the children in his arms, placed his hands on them and blessed them.

For Levi.
Praying you'll believe in God's love for you,
no matter what others say, as these children did.

S. W.

≳Little me≲
BIG GOD

Collect the series:

- The Man Who Would Not Be Quiet • Never Too Little
- The Best Thing To Do • The Boy Who Shared His Sandwich
- The Easter Fix • The Dad Who Never Gave Up
- The Little Man Whose Heart Grew Big

Never too little!
© Stephanie Williams, 2019.
Reprinted 2019, 2021, 2022.

Published by:
The Good Book Company

thegoodbook.com | thegoodbook.co.uk
thegoodbook.com.au | thegoodbook.co.nz | thegoodbook.co.in

Unless indicated, all Scripture references are taken from the Holy Bible, New International Version. Copyright © 2011 Biblica. Used by permission.

Stephanie Williams has asserted her right under the Copyright, Designs and Patents Act 1988 to be identified as the author and illustrator of this work.

ISBN: 9781784983697 | Printed in Turkey